THE UNSPOKEN

THE UNSPOKEN

What the World Don't Talk About

John L. Brown

To order additional copies of this book, contact:
Xlibris Corporation
1-888-795-4274
www.Xlibris.com
Orders@Xlibris.com
45518

INTRODUCTION

First, let me say, this book that you are about to read is not to put down the black man or woman or any other race. This book is factual. Some of the incidents you may be able to relate to. Please sit back and enjoy.

I wrote this book because I feel the people of the world should know how blacks from the ghetto are treated. Also, we as a people should not be victims of society. We should stand tall and hold hands throughout the world and say we will bring unity to all. I feel if we do, God will bring his special gift to the people of the world, and that special gift is peace. This book will not only portray the struggles of the black race but will also provide suggestions on how to pull ourselves out of the rut.

When we speak of rats, mice, roaches, drugs, run-down homes, overcharges at grocery stores, slum lords, no streetlights, potholes in the streets, liquor stores on just about every street corner, run-down schools without finances, welfare, substance abuse, drug dealers, and alcoholics on the corner, the list can go on and on. Why do our kids have to live like that? Where are the leaders? We never talk about our living condition in the ghetto. We go on with our lives as if it doesn't exist.

I can remember when I was a little boy: my family was working for peanuts. They were sharecroppers; I can remember that a white man used to come by the house and pick up money. One day, I overheard him tell my grandmother who raised me, "Dot, you need to make those boys work hard" (meaning her sons, my uncles and my father). They were robbed of their education because they had to work in the fields. These days we have learned that we have a choice. But with no education, they didn't have a choice. Either work or become a hobo. Have things become better since then? I don't think so. Think about it, things are worse. The crime rate in the ghetto is soaring. People are afraid to walk the streets at night; even in the daytime, they are afraid. Young black men and women are just too blind to see what is going on. That is why they are killing one another and going around scaring the older people. Young black men and women are dropping out of schools and colleges throughout the United States. Why? I think that it is because of the lack of knowledge and education. I keep saying, "What is going on?" I guess you are wondering, and I will get to that later in the book. Remember, we don't talk about these things to other races.

When I was eighteen years old, I went to join the U.S. Marine Corps. Why? To better myself. It turned out that the opposite happened to me mentally because of all the killing. I was a Marine Corps infantryman; I packed an M-16 and a mortar baseplate. I was a gunner for 60-mm mortar, which was a small artillery unit that could wipe out hundreds of people in just seconds. Our missions were to search and destroy. I had to pack my own food to last at least two weeks, five mortar rounds, ten magazine clips for my M-16, fully loaded extra rounds for my magazines, six canteens of water, my writing gear, dry socks, poncho, knife or bayonet, and other survival tools like maps, and etc. It was so hot in Vietnam in the summer, and the temperature could get up to 105 to 110 degrees. Every day we would spend all day searching for the enemy. We killed whatever enemy we would encounter that day. At night, we would dig our foxholes and rest for the night. This went on for months until I got hit. Many nights on watch,

I would look at the sky and wish that I was at home in my warm bed. I knew if I were home, I would be safe. Vietnam wasn't safe. Especially for those of us who were frontline marines. I had many close calls which I made it through by the grace of God. I will tell you two of them. Get yourself a cup of coffee or soda and hear these true stories.

FIRST STORY

One day around 10:00 a.m., we were around the area of the Ashow Valley when two men in our unit were killed. We called for the chopper. They took them off in body bags to be sent home. The rest of the day we looked, but we could not find any of the enemy. Later on that evening, we settled on top of the mountain. My friend and I decided to dig a foxhole together. As we were digging, the enemy attacked, and the mortar rounds were hitting all around our foxhole. My company commander yelled out, "Saddle up! We are pulling back." Everyone was to pull off the hill. My buddy and I couldn't go anywhere since the rounds were hitting all around our foxhole. When the rounds would hit, the dirt would fly on top of my shoulders, I could hear the scrap metal whispering by as the rounds were hitting so close. My friend was hit as he managed to get off the hill. Since I had to be left there by myself, in my mind I was so scared with all that was going on around me. When my friend got to safety, the unit asked him where I was. My friend told them that he thought that I was captured or dead. I stayed on the hill for about an hour by myself. It seemed like forever. I finally made it off. I saw one of the guys running to help me. The first thing they said was that they thought that I had died. I asked them where my friend was and was told that the chopper just left with him. They told me he would be all right. Then I started to cry since I thought that he had been killed trying to get off the hill. I think about it sometimes and say to myself, "Man, was I lucky." Also, I thank God.

SECOND STORY

One day, we were between mother ridge and the DMZ. My squad leader told us that we were going on a patrol, but we have to be alert because we were going into a "hot area." We went on, and as we were walking, we were ambushed by the enemy. We were hit hard. Then our squad leader called, "Mike, Mike up," which was my team. As we were fighting, I could hear the bullets whispering by my ears since they were so close. One of the other gunners on my team was killed right next to me. I yelled, "Corpsman up!" which means someone was hit. I rolled him over and he had blood coming out of his mouth. I didn't know what else that I could do, so I took over his position of gunner. That is when all hell broke loose. The rounds from the enemy were flying all round me. I could see the dirt flying where the bullets landed. All of a sudden, I saw this black thing flying in the air. When it hit, I put my hands to my face and my face and hands felt very hot. I looked at my hands, and they were full of blood. I thought I was going to die that day. I looked to one side and there were two other marines dead. I panicked and started to cry, "Corpsman up!" They called in a small bomber plane. When they were dropping, those bombs were so close to us that I could feel the heat and the scrap metal. Later, I found out that the black thing that I had seen was an "RPG" enemy round. I would never want to fight another war again. There isn't a day that goes by that I don't think about that place and all that happened there.

Now, I will tell you why I say, "They just don't know." In 1975, when the Vietnam War was over, the "reconstruction" of the black families began. I say this because the communities started breaking down. Black girls started having babies out of wedlock. The unemployment rate in the black communities hit its highest. Young black Vietnam veterans were left to their families' care, and black businesses started to close down. Most of all, black schools hit their poorest. The only people that I could see that this reconstruction of the black family helped were the "black politicians." The reason that I say this is because the black communities were left in the hands of the black community leaders. The bad thing of this is that they had "no power." They wanted to make things better, but they could not because there wasn't enough money in the black communities. I think we as a black race were abandoned and still are. Why? I can remember when I came out of Vietnam there wasn't any help for the veterans in the poor communities. I used to sit and stare at the walls, wondering what in the hell was wrong with me. My people didn't know what to do and neither did I. I moved from state to state looking for something to confront me, and I never could find it. I drank and used drugs for comfort as strange as that may sound. At that time, I was glad that I did because it kept me sane while things were getting out of hand for me.

Now, going back to the communities. The young blacks were also getting out of hand. They were killing one another for silly reasons. Families were splitting up. Hunger was hitting a record high in our communities. I can remember when I was growing up, people did not let one and another go hungry. If you were hungry, you could always get something to eat. It is as if we didn't care anymore for each other. We need to come together and help one another. We need to stop depending on the system.

AIDS has invaded our communities because of the lack of good health care education, and another thing, there are thousands of people in our communities across the United States with no health care programs. That I do blame the States, not the federal government. I think that the state should adopt a resolution for all the residents of that state to have at least a minimum help care program. Which is good dental care and regular vision checkups. The rate of which young girls are having babies has escalated. Studies shows that young girls between the age of fourteen and seventeen years are becoming pregnant by adult males. We don't know why these young girls are letting these adult males get them pregnant. We can assume that it could be that they are looking for someone to love. And some people say that they are having babies for the money. I think that this is happening more by rapes than anything else and that these males should be brought to justice. If we as a black race don't put a stop to it now, our young girls will have no future. Remember, these are some of the things we don't talk about in the communities.

I think that the most important situation that we are facing is the drug problem in the communities. I know of places were there are substance abuse centers on one corner and the dope dealers are on another corner. To me, it just doesn't make any sense. When I said, "Where are the leaders?" now you know what I am talking about. The police pass by the dope dealers and wave at them. Remember that this is going on in the black communities. Why? It seems to me that the black communities have been abandoned. I think the wealthy and some races think we are the scavengers of the human race. This is one of the reasons why we are having a drug problem in the black communities. The professionals say that because there aren't any jobs and people will do anything to feed their families. I say that's bologna because we have been treated as the scavengers of the human race since our people were brought here in chains. And in some of our minds we don't care about the human race. Them dope dealers know that drugs kill people; they just don't care. Black dope dealers look at our people as if we are nothing because they were taught to think that way. I say we need to take the communities back from them; to do so, we need help from our leaders.

I can remember when I was growing up in the South. If you were light skinned and had curly hair, you were a "good kid" no matter how bad you were. We were taught that to be black was bad. We ask ourselves, Have things changed? I don't think so. I did a survey of different stores. When I walked into the stores, the receptionist would be very light skinned if they were black. A very dark man is more likely to be accepted in our society than a very dark woman. It shouldn't be that way because I was taught that God made man in his image. But remember we were taught that black was bad. People say that was years ago, but it still have an effect and some races still believe it today.

We have to start teaching our kids that all men are created equal. Regardless of their color. Remember that there are light, dark, yellow, brown, and tan skinned people in this world and that we all started from one human being. Think about that for a while. Let us talk about getting back on track and stopping the nonsense.

First of all, mankind should know that God love all of us. And there is good and evil in our society. We should be able to distinguish between good and evil.

Let's talk about our black athletes in football, basketball, baseball, boxer, tennis, golf, and CEO of companies. That is to say anyone making over $200,000 a year. They can help the black communities. People say that they do, but the truth is, they don't. What they do is donate thousands of dollars to organization. Well, some organization doesn't help the poor struggling blacks. We need money for afternoon programs. Also, if they donate money in the black communities, we could create jobs for thousands of unemployed blacks. I am not saying don't help these organization or other nonprofit organizations but also to help your black communities.

There is plenty of work to be done as anyone knows the communities need money since no one wants to talk unless you have backing. So, black millionaires, start pooling your money together and start helping your black people if you want the respect of other races.

I think that our kids should start counseling and therapy at an early age before they enter elementary school. We should have a counselor at daycare centers to come in once a week to talk to the kids. Why? Because the majority of homes don't do this. For example, you take a single family home, the mother or the father work from nine to five. The parents are too tired to do anything after working besides cooking and making sure that the kids do their homework and bath. We have to start somewhere. Remember, we are talking about the black communities where there are drugs, violence, run-down homes, and apartments. These kids need hope.

Let's talk about the teenagers. Ask yourself the question, have we lost our teenagers? You might say yes, but I say no. Why? Because I think our teenagers' expectation of us as parents is beyond our wildest dreams, same thing with education. How many parents sit down and play video games with their kids, very few. Because most parents don't know anything about video games. Most counselors would say spend quality time with your kids, well, let me tell you something: that is their quality time. For girls, quality time used to be making cookies and cakes. Now it is listening to rap music, boys, and playing video games.

We have a problem all across America: about 25 percent of our kids won't attend school. We can't do anything about it until the federal government gives our strips back and changes the education system. Here is what I would do. First of all, the school system would make a survey on why the kids are not going to school. The problem with that is they give the survey to the kids that are going to school. I would give the survey to the kids who are not going to school. Also, I would come up with some kind of program for the schools and let the kids who are not going to school run it. That is one way to bring the kids back to school. If you know what I mean.

Let's talk about the black woman. Our sisters are having a rough time. Why, because I would say that in every fourth home and apartment in the United States there is a black woman with kids. Either she is raising the kids by herself, not married, the kids' father isn't there, or have another man living with her who isn't the kids' father. But the majority of the time she is taking care of the kid by herself. We ask ourselves why? Well, the black man have been beaten down. The black man has been talked about, lied too, have had the good-paying jobs taken away, and the sisters have left him stranded. The black woman will leave her baby's father for another man and later find out that man has a lot of issues too. These days in the course of a lifetime the black woman will have gone through at least twenty to twenty-five men and still be looking for mister right. Well, sisters, get it together because if you are raising boys, your son is going to try and find a woman just like his mom. Hard pill to swallow, but it's true. Let's get it clear: all sisters are not that way, just the majority.

I can remember when the black woman gave the black man the authority to lead the household, make the kids behaved, put food on the table, and money was not a big problem and the man took care of his wife and the wife took care of her husband. Things were better. Look at it now, the wife can't say anything to the husband and the husband can't say anything to the wife without a disagreement. Now, you can see the stress the black men and women are going through. I wonder who created that mess?

Let's talk about our brothers. There are a lot of sorry brothers. Lots of black men are getting young girls pregnant. How would they like it if that were their daughters? They would be ready to kill. But what is so cold is that they want take care of their kids. When the sisters go to the DA, they say that the sister is wrong. Guess what, no, she is not. Take care of your kids. Lots of brothers wonder why it is that the sisters are leaving them. They have stopped fighting back. A sister needs a warrior, not a quitter. Remember, brother, black people came from Africa and we were warriors and nothing has changed. Show a sister you are not a quitter. I'll show you a sister that will stick by your side.

Brothers, we have to go and get educated and come back strong. When I say this, I don't mean violence. We have to take back our kids from the streets. We have to take back our community. Our kids need us. We have to start showing leadership. If you are not working or on disability, start volunteering in the communities, the schools, charity programs for the kids. Brothers, that is working, do your part too.

When I started writing this book, I wasn't going to talk about what I'm about to say. Guess what, brothers and sisters, our communities are being invaded by Southeast Asians and Eastern people. They have taken over all the grocery stores, gas stations, hotels, beauty supply, nail shops; and they are renting and buying all vacant buildings in the communities. They use these buildings for trash. When you go into their places of business, they watch you like hawks, thinking that you are going to steal from them. Our kid can't get afternoon jobs because they won't hire them. We need to put a stop to it. It's all right to get a business in the communities, but they have to pour some of their money back into the communities.

One day I was at a corner store and I asked the store owner why he doesn't hire people from the community. He said that he doesn't make enough money. That is a lie because that store stays busy. These business owners in our communities don't put anything back into the communities. Here is what they do. They will give to the police department for their programs. But remember that this is hush money. The police forces throughout the United States are not working for the best interest of the black communities. They patrol the communities looking for trouble. Why can't they stop and talk to people and get to know the people in the communities? Also, get to know the kids?

Police officers could be a great asset to the black communities. Why? Because they come in contact with the blacks every day. Right now, they are hated in the communities because of all the harassment to the citizens. If only they would go into the communities to help these troubling blacks and be role models for them. Well, I know the crime rate will go down. The police officer is the only role model blacks have in the communities. I'm talking about on the streets. You don't find our athletes, CEO from companies, politicians, or anyone else coming in close contact with struggling blacks as do the police officers. There are some good police officers and they need to come together and help. This could make a difference.

I had to take a rest from writing and many things have happened since then. Our country has been attacked and has had many scares. They talk about terrorist attack. Black people have been attacked, and not just by airplanes. I'll tell you how, bad meat and food at the corner store, roaches, rats, mice in our homes or apartments, low-paying jobs, run-down school, liquor stores on just about every corner, and many more things. To blacks, this is what they call slow death. We have been living like this for so long we think that it is the way people have to live. Well no, it's not. Don't get me wrong; I don't approve of terrorist of any kind. I bring this up because the reader may be open to what's going on in the black communities. People may look at the news and they will never hear the reporters talking about terrorism in the black communities. Now you see what I mean when I say, "Black people have been abandon." Some people may read this book and say that the black communities are stronger than ever. That they have many programs, places to go, jobs, and many other things. Well, there are programs, jobs, places to go. The problems are if there are fifty slots open in the program, the friends and family members of the people working in the program get the slots. Do you see where I am going with this? Let us look at the programs in the communities and why they can't raise money for the community. In a city or country, there are many communities that have community leaders who never show their faces. The only time they do is when it is time to vote because they don't want to lose their paychecks. You can vote for anyone you want as your leader as long as they are on the ballot. We need leaders, not someone to keep you down. Let's look at the 9/11 attack; when that happened, people started pooling the money to help the victims. Why can't black people start pooling their money;

we also are victims. Don't you know that if we as blacks do start, then our kids will start to respect us. Other races will respect us. Most of all, we will start respecting ourselves.

Now let's get down to earth. In our community, we have places that really hurt us. Check cashing places that give payday loans, business that don't hire blacks. Only blacks in the community know what these businesses are. But we don't talk about that in our community because we are too busy struggling. Dope houses, business that makes the community look like a run-down liquor store.

Let's start with the payday loan places; I know many people got messed around with these places. Poor people go to these places and get a loan and they become in worse shape than before. These places are loan sharks in my eyesight. Any time you borrow $255, you have to pay back $300 in two weeks or a month is bad. Our leaders is letting these business rip us off. If you don't or can't pay them back, they call your home, employment, or family members and tell your business in a way that they are not violating the law, or they will tell you to just pay the interest on the loan which is $45. But remember, you still owe the $300 in two weeks. So for that month, you paid $90 in interest in one month for $255. That is ripping you off.

Stay away from these places. I think the federal government should step in and regulate these places. If you lose your job and can't pay, they don't make arrangements. So they send you to a collection agency for $300. Now your credit gets a mark on it.

The reason I am talking about this is we don't talk about payday loans. I think most people are ashamed because they have to get a payday loan. Let me tell you, don't be ashamed because we are being redlined in the black community.

No one will help us. That's why I say we need to pool our money together and create jobs so we can get out of this mess.

Let's talk about housing (rent). Rent is so high it's a shame. These run-down places is not worth the money; our leaders don't care. I would say over 50 percent of blacks living in the black communities have an eviction on their record. Why, because they don't make enough money to pay their rent. Landlords are just trying to make a profit. They are just to greedy they don't care about if you have a place to live; all they want is money. I've been in rentals where the toilet don't work, water is dripping from the kitchen sink. No weather stripping, weeds have taken over the grounds, broken windows, and the list can go on. It's bad, and where are our leaders. Most landlords think less of black tenants; they think that blacks is not going to take care of their places, but let me be clear. Blacks are not less, and we will take care of our living area. Blacks have a hard time getting a really nice place to live because of what people think about us.

Other races of people have lied about blacks by saying we are nasty, dumb, stinky, stupid, liars, grew tails at night, can't be trusted, we steal, anything negative they can say.

We are not that way at all. We as blacks are loving, caring, honest; and when we have a friend, we love that friend.

People of the world should start caring for each other. Stop bad-mouthing.

Business in the community that don't hire blacks, whoever read this short story, go in the black community and stop in on some of the liquor stores, corner store, gas station, community hotel or motel. Ask how many blacks work for them; you will be surprised what you will find out. Young blacks used to be able to get a job at McDonald's, Burger King, or Jack in the Box. But not anymore, the Mexicans took over those jobs. The Chinese and Japanese restaurants in the community, they will not hire a black person. Just go in the black community and find out for yourself.

I am not saying these people are racist or are prejudiced; they just don't hire blacks.

Remember, we don't talk about these things in our community. Because we feel that's just how it is, but it shouldn't be that way.

Let's talk about our legal system. I took my son to court for a traffic ticket. I was shocked by what I saw. About 95 percent of the people in the courtroom were blacks and the age limit was about eighteen to thirty years of age. Now they talk about racial profiling. I wonder what is going on in the judge's mind, is he comfortable with this situation? I wonder what would happen if our leader would investigate the police department in that city. My son were found not guilty of the ticket.

Brothers and sisters, we need to see what's going on with our kids because when I was in that courtroom, only about three parents were with their kids. The courts will railroad your kids into jail or prison.

Let me tell you that jail or prisons make slaves out of people. They work for 20¢ to 50¢ an hour. For large manufactories, making them rich, I know this book is controversial. Some people may say that's not true. Remember, the things I say and see is through my eyes and mind.

Scams in the black community, yes, it's plenty of them. Some of these scams are legal. Example, these credit card business—they target poor people. They offer them $250 line of credit. By the time they take out processing, membership insurance, and who knows what else, they have maybe $75 or $50 left. They say that the card will help your credit if you pay on time. The problem is you can't even rent a car or motel with the card because the card max is only $250. They are no better than the payday loan people.

I remember when I got scam. These three people came to my home and said they were from this organization called help. They were taking donations. The money were to help the poor people in the community across the United States. I gave them $20. Later, I found out they were scamming. They got busted.

The biggest scam in the community is panhandling. I know people go in front of McDonald's, stores, corners, anywhere there is a flow of people, and ask for money. These people make plenty of money. The signs they have makes you feel bad for them. I'll work for food, everyone needs a little help sometimes, homeless veteran, hungry, thank you and God bless. These people need to stop the nonsense. It's all right for people in need to ask.

Another scam (well, I will call a scam) is Goodwill, Salvation Army, secondhand clothing and furniture. These outlets get clothes and furniture for free and sell for a profit.

I always thought that they were to help the poor. That's not true. Salvation Army, I have a lot of respect for them. But they still need to tighten up. Don't wait until people got their lights turned off or get kicked out their house to help.

I was talking with a friend one day, he said, "(Man) I read your transcript of your book. It's right on target, before you publish your book you need to go back and talk about more thing that we don't talk about. Your book *The Unspoken* should be a bestseller. I hope it will make in the public stands."

Let's talk about health problems in the community. There are people in our community walking around with VD, herpes, AIDS, walking pneumonia, diseases that spread from one human being to another. Lots of them don't know they have these diseases till it's too late.

When family members get these diseases, the family keep it hush-hush, especially AIDS. If a family member has AIDS, they keep it hush-hush because they are ashamed of what people may say. Black fathers don't want their sons to be labeled as gays. That's a put-down for the family.

Well, we can stop all this by giving affordable health care. You will be surprised of the people in the black community that don't have health care.

People's teeth are falling out because they don't have dental ins. We don't talk about these things in the black community. We are to busy struggling.

I know some people want to live without struggling, but when you can't get a job that pays a wage that makes you afford health care, get a decent apartment or house, put good food on the table, it will always be a problem.

Some people are afraid of starting community meeting to combat these problems because if we tell it like it is, we will be labeled as mess makers; the problem is our leader want to fix the problem their way, but their way has failed.

They send the police in the community to fight drug sales, that's good and dandy. What they need to do is send the police to find out why these businesses don't hire blacks. The majority of people in the (ghetto) black community that sell these drugs are kids ages fourteen to twenty-five years old. They do this because they can't get no job in the community.

Some people may say that's not true, but I say it's true. Look for yourself.

I would say about 60 percent or higher of blacks in the black community have a record or in jail or have been to jail. For selling illegal drugs. Some people might say I am crazy because of what I am about to say. I think the federal government should go over the young people's records and pardon some and get that mess off their record. Why, because the drugs was a setup to keep the black community down. Whoever put the drugs in the community knew that there was no jobs for these young kids. People might say where is my proof, where did I get my information from. I got my information by living in the mix of things. No one told me this; I see it every day. Young black men and women can't get good jobs because of their records. It's a shame for our government to let these things go on.

Black people, we better watch out because one day we will wake up and say where are all the young black men. They will be dead or in prison. We have to do something about this mess we are in.

I am trying my very best to tell the world we need help in our community. Now it's up to us to make a positive change for our black people.

I don't want to sound as though I am leaving out the other races of people that's struggling, but blacks have been down too long. I know that there are whites, Mexicans, and other races of people living in the black community that are struggling but if we get help they will get help too.

I live in California, and what I see going on in the black community is a shame. If there's work going on, especially on the streets, the Mexicans get the job. If there is yard work to be done, the Mexicans get the job. If there is housework to be done, the Mexicans get the job. It's like where is the black men and women working at. Well, guess what, the majority of black men and women in the black community are not working. It's like blacks can't get a job. If anyone who read this book think I am just blowing wind, check it out for yourself.

The Mexicans, if they have a business, they will not hire a black; they only hire their own people. They need to hire other races of people also. Now, maybe I missed something. But what I've seen, I have never seen a black working for a Mexican doing yard work or construction.

We as blacks if we have a business, we are ready to hire all races of people. I think that's good. But we need to hire more of our black people, especially the struggling blacks. The majority of blacks who have. I think they try and make themselves look good by not hiring their own people. One thing they don't know is they are not respected by blacks and no other race of people. In the black community, we don't talk about these things. We walk to the store and see construction going on and see know one of our kind working on that street project. We keep walking as though we don't see. Gangs in the community, the reason they have gangs is a sense of belonging. These kids don't have any role model.

We as blacks have let our kids down. It's like we don't care about them. Some people may say that we don't know how to raise the kids of today. Don't believe that, things have not changed to raise a child; there is no formula to raise a child. Go back to the days when grandmother and grandfather made us listen to them. My mother died when I was six months old and my family raised me. When I did something that they thought was wrong, I caught a good whipping.

These days, people don't whip their kids because they are afraid of going to jail. That is why I say we have failed our kids. We need to whip them (don't abuse them), show them we love them. We have to save our children.

The black people is very talented. If we as parents bring these talents to surface in our kids, they will be respected and us as blacks will be respected. We have to get back to basics and explore our talent. We are good with sports, dancing, comedy, with our hands, anything with the hands. Boxing, carpentry, plumbing, roofing, barbering, hairdressing, taking care of yards, and many other things; but we don't tell our kids these things. I am not saying we are not good at working in offices or make good professions.

I am saying let's start getting our kids in building and trades and things we are good at.

I know some people who read this book may say what is this guy talking about, they have blacks in the building and trades. Well, they do. But check for yourself: very few young blacks are in that field. Why, because over 50 percent of them have a record and can't get in these high-paying jobs. When I said the government should step in and review those young people's records, that is why I said that.

During the Vietnam War, the government pardoned those who refused to fight or go in the military. If they can do this for these people, they can help these young black men and women get their lives back. These days you need a driver's license and a clean record to get in some of those programs and get federal grants for college. Some of those young blacks really try and get turned down. So they go right back to using or selling drugs; they end up dead or in jail.

Our black entertainer can make a big difference also. For example, your rappers, those guys make millions of dollars. They need to pump money in the black community to help. They have to remember that we as blacks made them rich. I am happy for them to make it out the hood. But don't forget where you came from. I wonder what would happen if the rappers get together and start rapping about the brothers and sisters to stop the gangs, go to college or get a trade, finish high school, respect your mother and father, respect the law, get the drugs out of the community, love and teach one another, what would happen.

I think the young people will listen to them and start getting themselves together. Also, the rapper should go in the communities and schools in the black community and talk to some of the young people. Be a positive role model. I have never seen them do that. They will probably say we do go in the community, but ask yourself, have you made a difference?

We have to start caring for the elderly in the community. Don't you know that some of our elderly black people barely eat? They get their social security check once a month after they pay their high rent; they don't have money for food. Either pay rent or buy food. They pay their rent because they are too proud to sleep on the street. This is the truth, the elderly people is barely making a living. Lots of them have to buy their own meds and they don't have money.

Also, they have doctor's appointments they can't get to. They do have vans to go around and pick up the elderly, but it's on a first-come-first-serve basis. So some get left out. When I see my black elders suffering because they can't get food or medicine, I feel really bad. I do help as much as I can by giving them rides when they need to go somewhere, but gas is so high I can't do it all the time. That's why I say we need to come together as blacks and start taking care of our own and stop depending on the system. Another thing we need to do in the community is to visit our elderly, let them know that we can be trusted and we care. We don't talk about helping the elderly. Let's start.

Now you can see why I named my book *The Unspoken*. Everything I put in this book is how it is in the black community. No one told me and I didn't have to get information from no one. These are some of the things that goes on, and we never talk about it. We go on with our lives as if it don't exist.

When I say liquor stores on just about every corner in the black community, well guess what, church's on just about every other corner on the main streets. Some of these churches are okay.

But the majority I don't know is why are they there. Don't get me wrong because I do believe in God and I believed that Jesus died for our sins. But some of those churches are not right. I've been to a few of them, that's all they do—down the young black people.

I want you to know many of the churches: their pastors are ex-alcoholic, ex-doper, ex-convict, and ex-prisoner. So how can they stand behind the pulpit and down another human being? What makes it so cold they actually believe themselves. I went to a church down the street from where I live. When I got in the church, they only had no more than seven people in the church for service.

Something is wrong with that picture. The people were very friendly, but I didn't go back because I felt a bad vibe. How can you have a church and only seven people show up on a Sunday for service?

I believe in churches in the community as long as they are serving a purpose for the community, such as being role models for everyone in the community not just their members. You know, black people, well, most of us are very spiritual. For some reason, we don't get away from being spiritual. When I was growing up, I was afraid of what was going to happen to me by God if I was to break the Ten Commandments. I can remember my grandmother saying, don't be bad because God was going to punish us (meaning, the kid), God don't sleep, my mother was going to pull my toes if I be bad. They put the fear of God in us. Well, if the church teach the basic, well, I think the community can get strong.

Now, we know there are things in the black community that we don't approve of, but we got to ask ourselves how we can better our standard of living. Well, here is one suggestion: let's start having healing meetings. Let's start talking about the things that we think that's life. As long as these things go on and we look at it as that's life, well, it will keep going on.

Since the church is in the community, go and ask the pastor, can you hold a community meeting? Find a creative way to attract the people you will invite. One way is food and gifts.

When I say the struggling blacks are abandoned, I say this because of what I see. Example, I was raised in Lake Charles, Louisiana. I go home at least every two years. It's depressing to see the black community that I grew up in. It's like a war zone. The houses look run-down. The paint is peeling. They still have people living in those sharpshooter houses that's about to fall down. The brothers and sister think it's okay and that's life. To me, that is not life; that's abandonment. Just about all the gas station and corner store have been taken over by other races of people. When I grew up in Lake Charles, there were no other race of people but black and white. The majority of all the store and businesses was owned by whites. Not anymore. Don't get me wrong, I am not saying the other race don't deserve an opportunity. But what about the blacks. Give us that loan to start our own. When we do go and apply for a loan, it's always something wrong. The banks will try and find a way not to loan us the money. You had an eviction or repression or outstanding check, you owe child support, you owe the courts for a ticket, you owe a payday loan, you're behind your rent or mortgage. The banks will find a way. Here is a good one. The area is a risk. But they will give other races a loan to start them a business in the same area where they turned you down.

Now I want everyone to read this book because some people don't know that these things exist. Some of your wealthy black people may say here is another black complaining, but remember, the only black person will say this is those that don't care and trying very hard to show other races of people that he or she have turned the other cheek.

Also, these blacks that have abandoned their own kind is not respected by no other race of people. And when they really need their black people, they will be abandoned. I am quite sure that we all know a few of these people.

I talk about other races of people that have invaded our community. I say this because of their action. I must say one thing, the whites are the only people that will try and help as little as they do but still they are doing something. The Arab, the Chinese, Japanese, Korean, Vietnamese, Mexican, Indian—it's like they don't care how much blacks struggle. They have their business in our community. They make plenty of money. They don't say how can I help these struggling blacks, and our leader let them get away with it. It is a sad situation.

I wish one day our leader will be brave enough to come to the black communities and see for himself. How this is a serious situation.

People may say how they can help or they can't do nothing. But I say they can. They can help by being role models themselves. They can give money to the communities that will help the struggling blacks.

Most of all, hear this, some people may say this guy is really nuts. Well, maybe I am, but this is how I see it through my eyes and mind.

The black community or the ghetto we can stop calling it that; why, because all races of people live in the community now. But we will always call it the hood.

Let's say if these people volunteer their time in the community to learn other people in the community, their culture and how to speak their language. Readers, can you see where I am going with this? They have all these nationality of people living in the black communities.

They are like strangers, also it's like their people have kicked them to the curb. They are very afraid also and they are confused. Well, let's say we all live together now and be friends, but you still have to contribute because if we struggling blacks get help, the other races will get help also. These pictures I am about to show in my book are very meaningful. They represent how the blacks live in the black communities and how the rich or advantaged live in their community. Is it fair, or ask yourself, have everyone has the same opportunity? After reading this book, I wonder what your answer will be.

Let's take a stroll were good people struggle every day to make a meal. They have to collect cans on the street and out the garbage cans to survive. Now, I must say some of these people do have jobs but are barely making it. And remember, I lived in a community just like these.

I live there because it captured some of the moment of Vietnam. As a combat veteran, it gave me a rush to hear the gunshots at night. Sometimes I had to rush for cover just in case of a stray bullet.

For many years, I saw these things go on in the black community and I have to talk about it. I hope my readers don't think I am being too hard because I am not trying to step on anyone's toes. I am hoping the world will wake up and start helping the struggling black communities. We need a helping hand from all races of people.

This picture was taken in the community at a trailer park. If you would walk in the trailer park, it would look like a bomb hit it. It has trash all over the place, hole in the parks, streets; and people live there trying to survive.

This picture is an abandoned or neglected piece of property; it's dirty, with grass growing wild, and the street is not being clean as you can see. I guess the city has come and covered the cracks and potholes.

This piece of property is an open lot and a house on it. The house, someone lives there; they have broken windows with a board covering the window, and it seems like no one cared for the lawn properly.

This property is a trailer lot; as you can see, someone is trying to sell the trailer. This lot is terrible.

This building looks bad. It's the people doing business in that building. This building just makes the community look bad.

This building was a church in the community; this is a very old building. They have a For Sale sign on it. It makes the community look bad.

This is a street in the community; the road is bad. Now, there are streets in worse condition than this road, but I just wanted to show a sample.

This is a very interesting house. The people have trash outside, in the yard is trash as the city is not collecting the trash. Maybe they are having hard times and can't pay for pickup service. Now you have seen the proof. Ask yourself, will our leader let this go on in their community? They were put in power to fight for the people, who can't fight for themselves, I thought. Now you can see when I say, where are our leaders and why do our kids have to see and live like this.

Now let's take a stroll in the rich and advantaged community. These people get good jobs which are high paying. To talk a little about the people who live in those community: They bring clothes, furniture, bed, silverware, dishes to Goodwill, Salvation Army, and other secondhand stores to help. That's a good thing, but what they don't realize is these secondhand stores sell those items sometime at a price where the poor people can't afford.

I have seen with my own eyes where stuff will be in the secondhand store for months. If they can't sell it, they will throw it away to the dump. Now, I don't think that's right because they could give that stuff away to poor struggling people. They received the item for free, why not give it away?

Also, some of these people will give money to different organizations, but the money never get to the poor struggling people. Some people may say that's not true. Well, do like I did—find out for yourself. But at least these people are trying. Those who makes an effort shows that their heart is not hardened and they have love for mankind.

This is a very beautiful home in the community. The streets are very clean. No liquor store on the corner and no pothole on the streets. People can sleep in peace.

This is a gated community—it's beautiful. There is no one standing outside the gate trying to sell drugs. The streets are clean. I guess if you get caught inside the gate, you will get questioned on who you are going to see. These people live good.

This is a beautiful community; the streets are so clean you can almost eat on it. The homes are beautiful. The police is making sure there are no intruders. When I was taking the pictures, the police followed me right out of their community. But I don't blame them. They were just making sure that those people are safe.

This is their community park. The grass is green, the lawn is taken care of; what amazed me is that they have the American, community, and POW flags flying. You don't see that in the black community, our parks are bad. They honor their veterans.

I bet you if you would ask a young black kid from the black community or ghetto what a POW flag looks like; nine times out of ten, they will say I don't know. Because no one honors black Vietnam vets, especially black people. That's the truth.

Let's talk about the heroes in the black community. There are many heroes, Vietnam vets. Some of these vets have earned Purple Heart, Bronze Star, Silver Star, and many other medals for serving in the military.

Plenty of these vets are homeless, sick, and can't get jobs. These guys and ladies have lost faith in our government. No one comes in the black community and try to seek out the vet. It's like they have been abandoned.

If you turn on your TV, if they are interviewing a Vietnam vet, well, you might see one black. Sometimes none. Well, as a combat vet, I fought right on the side of many blacks. I brought this up because as a struggling black, we should get recognition. Because we fought that war also.

I don't want no one to misunderstand me; I know there are other nationalities who fought the Vietnam War. But this book is mainly about the struggling black. But deep inside me, I feel everyone who fought the Vietnam War should get recognition. And if you fought the war, I don't care what race, rich or poor, you are still my brother. We made it back home. Now there are many other blacks in the community that are heroes. Your nurses, your retired worker that can't make ends meet. Your nurse aides, some of these people work in nursing homes, taking care of the elderly for very small wages. These are struggling good people that feel they will never get ahead.

These people are heroes because it takes a very special person that is warmhearted to do this kind of work for a small wage. These people are strong-minded to see their patient die, sick and can't do anything for themselves. I really admire these people.

There are your retirees in the black community that work all their lives, came from the cotton field down South to retire on a fair job and find out they can't live on their retirement. I go in the grocery store and see these people picking over food, trying to find something to eat that they can afford. They end up buying unnutritious food to eat. I say these people are heroes because they volunteer at food banks, churches that help the community with food, schools, and help with babysitting. Also, I see some of those people in the community trying to help the stressed and struggling teens stay in line. Now there are your teachers trying to teach kids in run-down schools and coming from dysfunctional families. Some people may say that's their job, but people don't know what these teachers go through. These teachers are truly heroes in my eyesight. I can imagine how good they feel when they see these kids graduate from school. Some people may say how he did know these things. Well, I was president for the school site council at one of the school in Oakland, California. And I have seen with my own eyes these teachers take trouble kids and make responsible adults out of them. Everyone pitched in. From the yard supervisor to the principal.

I mention the heroes in the black community because the world should know that not only we have been forgotten, but there are blacks in the community also that care and should be recognized—but we still need help.

There are other people in the community that we don't talk about—the murderers, rapists, thieves, and many other bad people. The advantaged fight to keep these people out of their community. These people have to live somewhere so they send them in our community. Remember what I said earlier in the book. There's good and evil in this world. For some reason, we end up with both in our community. They say people change. Well, if people change, why don't they let the rapists, murderers, and thieves live in their community? I know why because they don't want to stress over these people. So it's better us than them. We never talk about this situation. Believe this or not, these people get out of prison and recruit our young kids to sell drugs for them and do many bad things. They do this because they can't get jobs. Remember what I say there are no jobs in the black community for young struggling blacks so they go to work for these people?

Black brothers and sisters, let's start telling our kids they don't have to do that. Let's start supporting our kids.

Brothers and sisters, let's start teaching our kids the right way. How many of us talk to our kids about the Ten Commandments? What about the civil law and how to build a solid future for themselves? We all want good things for our kids, so let's get busy. I talked to many young and older people about my book. Well, I got a good response from all races of people about my book. This older lady told me that she had never touched a black person until she was about forty years of age. She said she always thought that black people were different; later in life she found out that we are all the same. She was glad that someone is writing about blacks' struggles and how blacks are treated in the ghettos. She said that many nationalities see it in the movies but do not realize that these things are really going on. I talked to this Korean lady; she told me that she married a black soldier and had kids. Her mother and father have never seen their grandkids and don't want to see them. When she told me her story, chills went through my body. I talked to this white lady; she told me that she went with her son to court. When the judge called her son's name to read the charges, she went with him. The district attorney asked her, was that her boyfriend because her son is white and black but he looks black? She said she told him that was her son. He was embarrassed. The reason I put this in my book is to let the blacks know that we are not the only people that have problems and we need to move on. And remember what I said earlier in the book. I am not trying to put down the black man or black woman and other races or people. But someone has to talk about these things. I guess you want to know what I am doing to combat the problem in the community. I am talking to all the unions to help the struggling blacks get in the unions. Many young blacks don't want to go to college. I talked to them about building and trade. I've helped a few young blacks, but I am doing this all by myself; also, I am using my own money for gas and paperwork. I am disabled and its rough, but I am trying. If only the rich blacks can see that there is a need in the black community, things can be better. I do know that some blacks help, but we need every black person across America to pitch in. Don't you know that if every black man and woman do their part in helping, there would not be any poverty among blacks? I hope that my book will bring some kind of unity among people of all races. These are some of the things that we don't talk about in our community.

Remember what I said early in the book: we are warriors, not quitters. We can all stand tall and be proud.

I talked about a lot of things. We as blacks are proud and strong. We should stay that way. We can't quit now. Our kids and older people need us. Also when we get ourselves together, we can help other races of people. We can be a role model for them.

I will close by saying that I love all people because no man is better than I am and I'm not better than anyone else. God made all of us.

Thank for reading.

Hope you will find happiness and peace.

INDEX

A

AIDS (acquired immunodeficiency syndrome), 16, 31
Arabs, 42

B

black communities. *See also* ghettos
blacks, 7, 18, 63
  as talented people, 37
  athletes, 18
  communities, 15, 18, 23, 43, 44, 59, 61
  elderly, 37
  families, 14
  men and women, 8, 22, 33, 36

C

Chinese, 28, 42
corpsman, 13

D

dope dealers, 17
drug problem, 16

F

federal government, 16, 20, 27, 33
foxholes, 9, 11

G

ghettos, 8, 32, 43, 58, 61
Goodwill, 31, 53